HOUGHTON MIFFLIN
Reading
A Legacy of Literacy

HEROES

HOUGHTON MIFFLIN   BOSTON • MORRIS PLAINS, NJ

California • Colorado • Georgia • Illinois • New Jersey • Texas

Design, Art Management and Page Production: Kirchoff/Wohlberg, Inc.

ILLUSTRATION CREDITS
4-21 Kevin Beilfuss. **22-40** John Hovell.

PHOTOGRAPHY CREDITS
22 Photofest. **23** Photofest. **24** Stanley Dance. **24-5** Corbis/Bettmann.
26-7 Photofest. **27** Corbis/Bettmann. **28** Underwood & Underwood/
Corbis. **29** Corbis/Bettmann. **30** Michael Ochs Archives, Venice CA.
30-1 Frank Driggs/Archive Photos. **32** Charles Harris/Pittsburgh Courier/
Corbis. **33** Corbis/Bettmann. **34** Hulton-Deutsch Collection/Corbis.
35 AP/Wide World Photos. **36** AP/Wide World Photos. **37** Lynn
Goldsmith/Corbis. **38** Gjon Mili/Life Magazine © Time, Inc. **39** Corbis/
Bettmann. **40** AP/Wide World Photos. **40** (i) AFP/Corbis. **41** AP/Wide
World Photos. **42** AP/Wide World Photos. **43** Corbis/Bettmann. **44** AP/
Wide World Photos. **45** PhotoDisc. **46** Jacqueline Duvoisin/Sports
Illustrated © Time, Inc. **47** © 1987 Leaf, Inc. **48** Don Smith/Allsport.
49 Richard Mackson/Sports Illustrated © Time, Inc. **50** VJ Lovero/Sports
Illustrated © Time, Inc. **51** John Biever/Sports Illustrated © Time, Inc.
52 John Biever/Sports Illustrated © Time, Inc. **53** Peter Read Miller/Life
Magazine © Time Inc. **54** AP/Wide World Photos. **55** AFP/Corbis.
56 (bkgd) AP/Wide World Photos. **56** AFP/Corbis. **57** (t) AP/Wide World
Photos. **57** (b) National Baseball Hall Of Fame Library, Cooperstown NY.

Printed in U.S.A.

ISBN: 0-618-04402-7

13 14 - VH - 06 05 04

HEROES

Contents

▶ **Thanks to Sandra Cisneros** . . . **4**
 by Daniel Santacruz
 illustrated by Kevin Beilfuss

▶ **Duke Ellington:**
 A Life in Music **22**
 by Erick Montgomery
 illustrated by John Hovell

▶ **Mark McGwire:**
 Home Run Hero **40**
 by Richard Merchant
 illustrated by John Hovell

Thanks to
Sandra Cisneros

by Daniel Santacruz

illustrated by
Kevin Beilfus

Strategy Focus

What will help Miguel finally write his first
poem? As you read, try to **predict** what
will happen as Miguel learns about a
famous poet.

Mr. Shaw closed his book and got up from his desk. English class was ending. "Tonight," he told the class, "I want you to write a poem."

"A poem?" Miguel gulped and made a face.

"Yes, Miguel. A poem," said Mr. Shaw. "It can be about anything. You can even write about your sister if you want to."

"A poem about my sister," Miguel laughed to himself. "Who would want to read that?"

When Miguel got home after school, he sat down at his desk. He started to think about the poem. It made him feel nervous. "What can I write a poem about?" Miguel said to himself.

Miguel loved stories, especially mysteries and books with lots of action. But poems were different. The only poems he knew were about flowers or sunsets and things like that. And he lived in the city. What did he know about flowers and sunsets?

Miguel tried to write a poem several times. But each time he started, he stopped before he had finished the first line. It made him feel mad. He crumpled up the piece of paper and tossed it into the garbage pail next to his desk. By now it was filled with white balls of paper.

Finally, Miguel decided to do his math and spelling homework. He would give the poem another try after dinner.

When dinner was over, Miguel sat at his desk again. He tried writing about a beautiful sunset he had seen over the lake when he had gone swimming last summer. He tried writing about the flowers he gave his Mom for her birthday. He even tried to write about his older sister Flora. But every try ended up in the garbage pail.

Just then, Miguel's sister Flora came into his room. "Need any help with your spelling or math?" she asked.

Miguel shook his head. "No, I finished that already. Now I have to write a poem."

"A poem about what?" she asked.

"That's just the problem. I don't know," Miguel said.

"Poems can be about anything," Flora said. "Just pick something."

"Don't they have to be about things like sunsets or flowers or love?" asked Miguel.

"Wait here a minute," Flora said. "I've got something I want to read to you." Then she ran out of the room.

A minute later Flora appeared again with a worn book in her hand. She quickly flipped through the pages until she came to the one she wanted. "Now listen to this poem. It's called 'Good Hot Dogs,'" she said.

"You mean like the things we eat?" Miguel asked, trying not to laugh.

"Exactly," she said.

Flora read the poem slowly. As she read,
a small smile spread across Miguel's mouth.
There were no sunsets or flowers in it. The poem
was just about eating hot dogs. It reminded him
of the Saturdays he and his family went to the
hot dog shop after shopping. Like the poet, he
too liked mustard and onions on his hot dog.
And he laughed when the poem talked about
eating even the little burned pieces of french fries.
He never left a piece on his plate!

When Flora finished reading the poem, she looked up at Miguel. He was smiling widely. "Do you see what I mean now?" she asked.

"Exactly," he replied. "By the way, who wrote the poem?"

"A poet by the name of Sandra Cisneros," Flora replied.

"Does she have other poems like that?"

"This book is full of them," she said. "You can borrow it."

Miguel asked his sister lots of questions about Sandra Cisneros. Her answers surprised him. He found out that she came from a Mexican family like theirs. Not only that, but she had been born in Chicago too. That's probably why he recognized so much in the poem about the hot dogs. Maybe they had even gone to the same hot dog shop.

Miguel also found out that many of Sandra Cisnero's books and poems were about her own experiences. She wrote about her family and friends and people she knew. And she wrote about other people whose families came from Mexico.

Flora read a few other poems to Miguel. He could see why his sister liked her poems so much. So many of them reminded him of himself and his family.

Flora also told him that when Sandra Cisneros was a child, she couldn't find any books or poems about people whose families were from Mexico. That's why she decided to write about them. She wanted her people to finally see stories and poems about people like themselves.

When Flora left his room, Miguel knew just what he was going to write about. He walked straight to his desk and grabbed a pencil. The words came easily to him now. He hardly even used his eraser. When he finished, he read the poem over again. He actually liked it!

Miguel took the poem to Flora's room. He handed it to her without saying a word. She started to read it.

I've written my first poem to you.
There will not be a poem number two.
You know I'd rather do addition
Than sit and write this composition.

But to you my sister Flora I write
Because you help me do homework at night.
So many spelling words you taught me,
And for the baseball cards you bought me.

I write to say I think you're fine.
I'm glad Flora is a sister of mine!

When Flora finished reading, she was smiling widely. "That's a nice poem," she said. Then she gave Miguel a hug.

Miguel smiled. Thanks to Flora and Sandra Cisneros, he now knew he could write poems after all.

Responding

Think About the Selection

1. Which of Sandra Cisneros's poems does Flora read to Miguel?

2. Why is hearing the Sandra Cisneros poem helpful for Miguel?

3. What makes Flora read the poem to Miguel?

Why It Happened

Copy the chart. Then fill it in for each event.

Cause	Effect
?	Miguel starts to feel nervous.
As a child, Sandra Cisneros couldn't find any books or poems about Mexican people.	?
?	Miguel finally writes a poem about Flora.

21

Duke Ellington:
A Life In Music

by Erick Montgomery

Strategy Focus

How did Duke Ellington change music in America? As you read, **monitor** your reading to make sure you're following the story. Reread any parts you need to **clarify**.

His real name was Edward, but his friends called him Duke. He was born in Washington D.C., in 1899. His talent for music took him far from there. People all over the world came to know Duke Ellington. They knew him for his wonderful, new music and his beautiful smile.

23

Left: Duke Ellington at age four.

Top: The Duke Ellington Orchestra in 1927.

Duke was seven when he began to play the piano. He liked to play *ragtime* music. Ragtime was a lively music that sounded strong and fast. Playing ragtime gave Duke his quick fingers. It got him thinking of music all the time. At the age of fourteen he wrote his first song, "Soda Fountain Rag."

Duke began to earn money playing with bands all over Washington. Then, when he was 24, he went to New York City. That's where his music really took off.

In New York, Duke started his own band, The
Duke Ellington Orchestra. An orchestra is a large
band with many players playing many different
instruments. Duke started his orchestra with
twelve players.

By 1927, the Orchestra was playing at
Harlem's famous Cotton Club. Duke played piano.
He led the band. He also wrote the music. Duke
had many big hits. The songs "Mood Indigo" and
"Sophisticated Lady" were two of the first.

The Duke Ellington Orchestra also played live
on the radio. That made it possible for people all
over to hear Duke's music.

Duke was making a new kind of music. He had the players in his band *improvise* as they played. When musicians improvise, they make things up as they play. People were not used to such a bold sound. The Duke Ellington Orchestra became famous for their improvised music.

Top: The Cotton Club in Harlem, New York City.

Left: Duke and his improvising Orchestra.

Duke's Orchestra played a fun, fresh kind of music that people loved. It surprised people. It made them move. This music had smooth sounds that thrilled listeners. It had jumpy sounds too.

Duke Ellington writes a song with Billy Strayhorn.

Duke Ellington was at his best when great musicians worked with him. One of the greatest was a songwriter named Billy Strayhorn. When Duke met Billy, Duke knew he had found someone special. Billy became Duke's musical partner in 1939. Over the next forty years, they wrote hundreds of songs together. One was "Take the 'A' Train." It became the Duke Ellington Orchestra's best-known song.

In the 1930s and early 1940s, big bands like Duke's were playing a kind of music called *swing*. It was music to tap your feet to. It was music to get up and dance to. People made up new dances to go with the music. The Duke Ellington Orchestra performed swing music all over the United States.

All over America, people danced to swing music.

On January 23, 1943, the Duke Ellington Orchestra played in Carnegie Hall in New York City. Few African Americans had ever played at this beautiful, world-famous concert hall. Duke Ellington had *composed*, or made up, a new song for this special event.

Top: Duke performs at Carnegie Hall.

Right: Duke gets ready for Carnegie Hall.

Duke and his band played his song. It was called "Black, Brown, and Beige." This was not music to dance to. It was a serious work for a big concert hall. Not everyone liked it. But Duke had always dreamed of making music that would tell the story of African Americans in a great way. With "Black, Brown, and Beige," Duke was making this dream come true.

Duke said that the music he wrote and played was "the voice of his people." And he took that music everywhere. It seemed that everyone who heard his music wanted to hear more and more.

Duke Ellington was famous for his energy. He never tired of writing music. When people asked him what his favorite song was, he liked to answer, "the next five coming up." He would keep writing songs for a long time to come.

Duke Ellington flashes his famous smile.

Duke's music was a bright light for U.S. soldiers in World War II.

From 1941 to 1945, the United States was fighting World War II. The Duke Ellington Orchestra helped to bring smiles to people's faces in a time of great sadness and worry. Soldiers could listen to his music and think about their families back home listening too. Duke's music was a bright light in a dark time.

Ella Fitzgerald sings a song.

It was not just the Duke Ellington Orchestra that people loved. People also wanted to hear the guest singers who sang with the Orchestra. Duke made sure that people got to hear the best. One singer was Ella Fitzgerald. Her singing was like no other. She used her voice as if it were an instrument.

Another famous player was Louis Armstrong. He was a gifted trumpet player. He sang too. His rough voice and his fantastic trumpet playing gave the Orchestra a New Orleans-style jazz sound. There was no one like Louis Armstrong, either!

Duke Ellington plays with Louis Armstrong.

President Richard Nixon presents Duke with the
Presidential Medal of Freedom.

In 1969, Duke Ellington was given the
Presidential Medal of Freedom. That honor is
given to special people for service to the United
States. Duke Ellington got his award for the years
of beautiful music he had given to his country.

Duke Ellington was the most famous jazz musician of his time. Maybe of all time. He changed popular American music. Musicians all over copied him. He gave them the courage to try new ways of playing and singing music. Even today, young musicians study Duke's music. They dream of someday being as good as Duke was.

Today, musicians like Wynton Marsalis still play Duke's music.

Most people who met Duke Ellington were surprised by how gentle he was. That quiet, elegant man made people happy all over the world. For 50 years, he led the Duke Ellington Orchestra. He made the music that still makes people want to listen, tap their feet, and dance.

Responding

Think About the Selection

1. Where and when was Duke Ellington born?

2. Why was it important in his career that Duke Ellington moved to New York City when he was 24?

3. Why do you think people loved Duke Ellington's Orchestra so much?

Making Judgments

Copy this chart on a piece of paper. Read the story clues and write a judgment about Duke Ellington.

Story Clue	Judgment
Duke Ellington wrote a new song to play at Carnegie Hall.	Duke knew that playing there required a special song.
With "Black, Brown and Beige," Duke was making his dream of telling the African American story come true.	?

MARK McGWIRE:
Home Run Hero

by Richard Merchant
illustrated by John Hovell

Strategy Focus

How did Mark McGwire become America's home run hero? As you read, **evaluate** the facts and opinions of this baseball giant.

It was September 8, 1998. The giant man in the St. Louis Cardinals uniform gently turned the baseball bat around and around. His huge arms made it look like a toothpick. His eyes were fixed on the Chicago Cubs' pitcher, waiting for the ball. Finally, the pitcher leaned back and threw.

Mark McGwire hits number 62!

CRACK! The baseball popped off the end of the bat and screamed towards the outfield. It looked as if the ball was going to bounce off the wall. But it kept going just enough to clear the wall — a home run! Everyone in the crowd jumped to their feet and started cheering wildly. It was the most exciting day of the 1998 season.

Roger Maris

The huge man who hit the ball was Mark
McGwire. It was his 62nd home run of the season.
He had hit far longer home runs that year. This one,
however, was the most important. This one broke
the record of 61 home runs in a season set by Roger
Maris in 1961. The great Babe Ruth held the record
before that with 60 home runs way back in 1927.

Mark was so excited that he almost forgot to touch first base! All of the ballplayers on the field congratulated him as he circled the bases. When he crossed home plate, he ran straight to his son Matthew. He lifted him up in the air in front of the cheering crowd. The usually calm Mark was grinning from ear to ear. He had just made the most famous hit in baseball history.

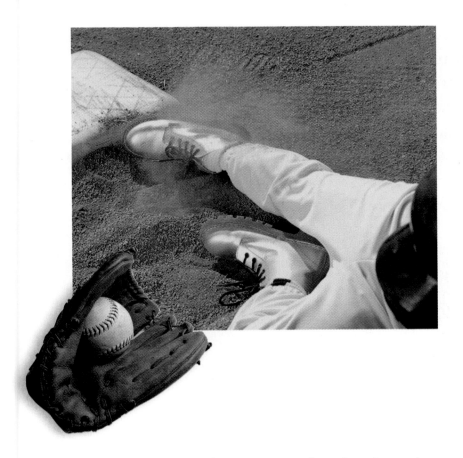

As Mark stood there, it was hard to imagine he had ever had problems playing baseball. Few people knew that while growing up, Mark's poor eyesight had caused him a lot of trouble. But even as a young boy, Mark was never one to let problems stand in his way. He just kept trying.

Mark played on the 1984 U.S. Olympic team.

Mark worked hard to make himself a star player in school. No one on his high school team worked harder. Later in college, he set the first of his home run records. The hard work paid off. He was chosen to play major league baseball by both the Oakland A's and New York Mets. Mark picked the A's so he could live closer to his family in California.

During his first full season in the majors, Mark made history right away. He hit 49 home runs to lead the American League! It was the most home runs ever hit by a player in his first year. Mark could have hit even more, but he decided not to play the last three games of the year. Instead he wanted to be at his son's birth. "You'll always have a chance to hit 50 home runs," Mark told reporters later.

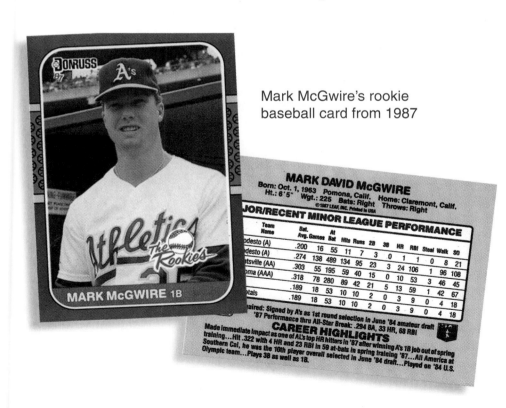

Mark McGwire's rookie baseball card from 1987

During Mark's first year, he was an all-star. Everyone expected him to get even better the next year. Maybe they made him nervous or maybe he tried too hard. But in his second year, he hit only 32 homers.

Mark struggled through his second year in the majors.

Even though Mark was still a good player, the fans and the press were disappointed. They wanted him to be a star. By the middle of the 1988 season, Mark started to become angry with reporters and fans. He thought they expected too much from such a young player. But inside Mark wanted to do better too.

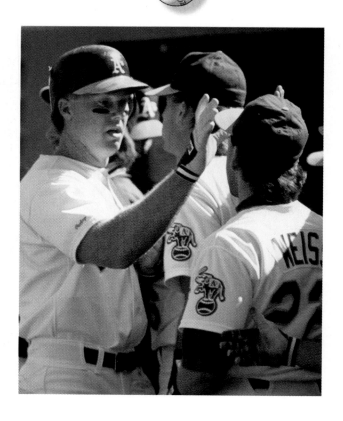

Mark tried to figure out how to become a better hitter. He tried standing closer to home plate. That meant he might get hit by a pitch. Mark thought it would make it easier for him to hit the ball.

Still his hitting kept getting worse. So did his vision. Other players and coaches tried to tell him what he was doing wrong. But nothing worked.

In 1992, things seemed to look up for Big Mac. He hit 42 home runs that year and started playing better. He was hoping the next year he would improve even more. But then he got injured and missed much of the season. He got injured again the next year too. Things were going from bad to worse.

By now Mark was thinking of quitting. Everyone thought he would never be as good as he had been. But while Mark was injured, he didn't give up. He began watching all the pitchers very carefully. He studied their pitches, hoping it would help him for the next season.

In 1995 Mark slammed 39 home runs. He did this even though he played only part of the season because of injuries. In 1996 he did even better, pounding 53 home runs. Now other pitchers were afraid of him. He was a star again.

Many fans wondered how Mark improved so much. He knew the answer. He had learned how to focus and concentrate.

Mark would need to focus all he could the next year. He started the season by hitting 34 homers for the A's. Then, on July 31, Mark was traded to the St. Louis Cardinals. Still, he kept hitting home runs. Now, it was getting harder for Mark to concentrate. Before and after each game, reporters hounded him with questions. "Will you break the record this year?" they asked. Mark came close. He hit 58 home runs that season.

The next year Mark started hitting a lot of home runs for the Cardinals. But now he had another problem. Sammy Sosa, a player for the Chicago Cubs, was also hitting a lot of home runs. All season long, they challenged each other for the league lead. Still, they stayed friendly. The competition made them both play better.

Sammy Sosa

Mark and Sammy Sosa both had great years in 1998. They both broke the existing home run record. But at the end of the season, Mark finally came out on top. He had hit an amazing 70 home runs. That record may never be broken. It shows what's possible if you work hard, stay focused, and don't give up.

Responding

Think About the Selection

1. On what date did Mark McGwire break Roger Maris's home run record?

2. What did Mark McGwire give up to be at his son's birth? Why do you think he did that?

3. "During Mark's first year, he was an all-star." Is this a fact or an opinion?

Fact and Opinion

Copy this chart on a piece of paper. Read the sentences from the story. Write whether the sentence is a fact or an opinion.

Clue	Fact or Opinion
He had just made the most famous hit in baseball history.	?
No one on his high school team worked harder.	?
In 1995 Mark slammed 39 home runs.	?